ABOUT THE AUTHC

Ellora Sutton is a poet ... ent based in Hampshire. She was the Poetry Boo ... ety Spring 2023 Pamphlet Choice with Antonyms for Burial (Fourteen Poems); her most recent pamphlet, Artisanal Slush, was published by VERVE. Her work has been published in *The Poetry Review, Magma, Oxford Poetry, The North, Propel, Berlin Lit,* etc., and she has won competitions including the Mslexia Poetry Competition and the Artlyst Art to Poetry Award. She has held the position of poet-in-residence at both Jane Austen's House and at Petersfield Museum and Art Gallery, the latter of which she is now proud to be a trustee of. She is the poetry reviewer for Mslexia, and the host of a popular monthly poetry night at her local indie bookshop, Goldfinch Books. Her PhD research uses poetry to explore how women experience museums as walkable urban spaces in London. She is at her happiest when wafting around an art gallery, or nibbling cake in a garden centre café. You can find her online at ellorasutton.com.

ABOUT *LITTLE BITCH*

'Sharp, tender, hilarious. Little Bitch *is a marvel! I am moved and changed reading it. Sutton takes us from raspberry ice cream to murdered girl-meat, oscillating between the brutal and beautiful, the candied and cruel, masterfully. 'Gorgeous, gorgeous, gorgeous'. I'm going to be shouting about this one from the rooftops.'* Rachel Long

'I imagine the words 'Little Bitch' *painted on the side of a bomb, falling from the sky, and I am giddy with envy that you are about to be in its crater, its explosion of smarts and sensuality and sincerity and other things beginning with s I can't think of right now because mostly what I want to say is 'astonishing astonishing astonishing, these poems, this brain, this openness to the world, and all the pain and pleasure within it', and if you do not feel that after reading this you and me cannot be friends.'* Rishi Dastidar

'I sometimes see poems described as 'playful', and it's simply a stand-in for a word that means anything but 'actively sombre' - these poems, however, are genuine acts of play, language games where a lyric I cavorts against the limits of how a self is permitted to self-narrate. Contemporary emphemera rubs up against canon, grief finds a shared vocabulary with sexual fluidity. Little Bitch *is a work of dynamism and scholarly rigour, daylight wit and desperation.'* Susannah Dickey

Little Bitch

Ellora Sutton

VERVE
POETRY PRESS
BIRMINGHAM

PUBLISHED BY VERVE POETRY PRESS
https://vervepoetrybookshop.com/vpp
mail@vervepoetryfestival.com

FIRST PUBLISHED APRIL 2026

Printed and bound in the UK
by ImprintDigital, Exeter

ISBN: 978-1-913917-93-7
EBOOK: 978-1-913917-94-4

Cover Image: Kaiya Bartholomew

For my mother, and the body she gave me.

CONTENTS

iii. Resurrection Myth, with Handcuffs

Little Bitch

'Your body / Hurts me as the world hurts God.'

—Sylvia Plath, 'Fever 103°'

'And what did I do with the rose? I did this: the rose was mine.'

—Clarice Lispector (trans. Rachel Klein), 'One Hundred Years of Forgiveness'

i. Wish You Were Here

Underglaze Blue

We are a Site of Special Scientific Interest.

After dark, the ice-cream parlour drips
like an abattoir; the deckchairs wait
patiently.

Everyone is haunted here.
We say it's the sea breeze
that exhausts us, but really
it's all this
spinning.

In the high season
there are ghost tours,
such magnificent ghost tours.

Sometimes they last for days, and I
do not sleep for the fullness—

this starry lung of water
consumptive with the dancing
of an entire tourism-dependent town.

I do not sleep for the bellyache of wishing
to howl into the harbour

I see you   you are more
than what you hold

I hold warm folded towels, dreams I never remember,
dreams that linger, that stick to my shoulders
like wet sand drying, the hands of a mother
ushering me on.

I dream in dead languages of contortion,
the cartography of homecoming in the sheets
after heavy overnight rain.

My iron gates have been unhinged, deboned,
repatriated with the wet earth. My body
fading to rope-burns, to shells and
cut-up glass and softened glass.

I just want somebody to grab my face as though raising me from the water. The tide is rising and my leg is stuck in the collapsed beams, the rubble, the double spring steel bear trap of

wade out to me, O moon,
O wet earth   dissolve this girl
like a wafer in your chapel-mouth
your scuffed kneelers your disputed
sheela na gigs

My body is not a house.
It is a broken-necked alley
leading down
to the quay—

palace

the water calls back

palace

palace

I don't want you to drown with me but say that you will. Pretend until I am gone. Tell me: we are living proof of light, you won't let me die, and I sing in my sleep, your girl, always singing

like the sea.

Concierge

After Children's Games *by Dorothea Tanning*

It's too late to catch the sunset
and too far to the dunes and I just
do not care. I am the girl on her back,
I am the girl eating her own hair.

I am the blonde having a tantrum
the way some girls my age are having babies.
I am having instant noodles. I'm in so deep,
I can't remember if I hate my body
or being told not to hate my body.

Fucking tourists, I actually *live* here.

I'm Venice in August, Disney World all year round.
How light scathes me. How I have scathed myself,
foraging through the after-dark for softer parts
in theme-park morgues—I am as much a woman
as I am a dream. My latest heart: the football
of a dog's overinflated head,
its blown-apart sense of joy. Everything
will be okay, and if not?
                                        Traffic—

All these flashes! I am a racoon
washing candyfloss in a stream, wondering
where the hell
all that sweetness went.

Thigh Slit

Last night I dreamt I was a flame
dancing for a pack of moths so huge
horses could have galloped
through their grey veins.

Like every dream of home
I was the market, a cosmos
of flies and impermanent
awnings, covered in flies
like a heart.

It was a sweaty, trough-like dark.

It was a dream that left me
overexposed and lost
in the menstrual wharf
of this dress—

a vast geranium
where a geranium
has no business being.

Cruel Beach

Dearest—

I wish you were here, where I am delicious and nothing, cud on the beach's tongue, too good to swallow. Here I am wild, and my wilderness is coastal: I am praised. My love, how far am I from home?

In my dissociations you *are* here, and you are weaving my hair into a vast net, but you never finish. I never know what kind of net you are turning me into. I want you to come over here and empty me.

The sea rattles her numerous white keys.

A child is watching me write this. A *child*. Cannibal with raspberry sauce. Her mother spits her clean. Cruel beach. The stones leave bruises but aren't sharp enough to make me bleed, make me part of the sea, fill me with the filthy guts of hovercrafts and cruise ships, run-off and ejaculate.

We all pass through each other, and each other, and again.

The sound of longing is an ice-cream van's alarm. I don't know that I'm not Jesus. I might be. I might be a little bit Jesus. I have cried myself sick wanting another flake, a snot of seaweed is touching me like a man would. Give me a sugar cone full of red sauce and rainbow sprinkles and a knuckle of pink bubblegum at the bottom just for choking on, just for me!

What will the headlines say?

Something autoerotic, something holy.

It is beautiful here. It is awfully peaceful. I want you here, I want to send you everything I touch, the hot sand under my thighs. I hope the ammonites reach you with their crazy eyes intact. Hold them until they are hot. Fist. Puck. Think of me, my knees, one over the other. The pier ballroom is boarded up but sometimes there is glass and I catch myself, inside, a tin mine in the lap of a fruit machine. Think of me like that, in all my silver finery, dancing into the sea. Think of my furs fanning out about me like a Virgin. The sea entering my body like a sword. I think I might be Jesus. I suffer like Jesus did.

I really do. Wish you were here.

Your most
Darling

Radioactive Pink

After Juno Calypso

All the flowers here are the same colour
and there are no weeds.
There is a pool, but it makes my eyes fizz.

The light here is toxic in newer, more exciting ways—
I catch glimpses of my potential
in the girl-shaped chemical burns on my palms,
the fraying edges of my pink silk kimono.
Bending over the kitchen counter,
I mistake myself for an ice-cream cake in the oven's dark vanity.

The water tastes like there are cherries
spoiling in the tank.

The worst thing to ever happen to me
happened so long ago
sometimes I question if it even happened to me
or if it's just a story I tell myself to justify all this
Black Forest gateau.

Can't I just go, be a graveside somewhere?
No beautiful women, no wailing. Just cats
stretching, scrapping, perfectly unaware
that I used to be in pain.

On Cute

Cute comes from *acute*, as in: *small*, as in: *sharp*, as in: *angle of less than 90°*. The first act of any child is, by necessity, an exit wound.

In 1872, Charles Darwin, after studying his own children, identified *cute* as the evolutionary instinct to protect, defend, savage, and maul. In evolutionary terms, only the cutest babies survive.

Acute can also mean *dire, dreadful, shrill,* or *cunning*.

One of the things my hometown is famous for: the murder of Fanny Adams, a Victorian schoolgirl killed and dismembered so horrifically that sailors in the navy started referring to their rations of tinned meat as *Sweet Fanny Adams*. Over time, this was shortened to *Sweet F. A.* which is now taken to mean *Sweet Fuck All*. I have never visited her grave, though I have a postcard of it. I can see her graveyard from my boyfriend's kitchen window. Sometimes, I imagine my boyfriend as a giant teddy bear with strong hands and a penis attachment.

The main project of cute might be said to be plausible deniability. Even a baby, who has no concept of manipulation, is cute with the evolutionary intention of manipulating its caregiver into feeding them, sometimes at great personal cost. In short: cute requires a sucker.

Hello Kitty isn't a cat, she's a little girl. Hello Kitty is five apples tall, and weighs three apples. She started life as a coin purse, and dreams of becoming a poet. Hello Kitty doesn't have a mouth, apart from when the product design requires it.

Nostalgia, like kitsch, falls within the fallout zone of cute. All memory is, to some extent, nostalgia. Isn't that crushing? That even your most brutal memories are, by definition, softened.

Animator Gyimah Gariba defines cuteness as *if you bite me, will I forgive you?*

I ask my boyfriend if he would still love me if I were a spoon. *What kind of spoon?* A tiny neon-pink plastic spoon, the kind you get with overpriced ice cream at the theatre, in the interval, before it all goes wrong.

See also: *domestication syndrome.*

Cute is a pill with (possible) side effects. My antidepressant is cute: it makes me markedly less likely to kill myself but also markedly less likely to cum. If it only did the former, it would be considered *sweet* rather than *cute.*

Cute tells me that my greatest power is how other people perceive my powerlessness. Cute as domino mask. Cute as riot shield, as lingerie. Men seem to fear me most when I shrink back and look up at them through my eyelashes. I think it's my hunger that scares them, their inability to look away. The realisation of what they are capable of.

Hello Kitty collaborated with SPAM to produce a musubi kit. Musubi is a popular snack of rice, fried SPAM, and nori, pressed together. The Hello Kitty SPAM Musubi Kit includes two twelve-ounce tins of SPAM Less Sodium (25% less sodium than SPAM Classic), and one plastic Hello Kitty mould (pink). This (pork, ham, mechanically separated chicken) is where Hello Kitty shakes hands with dismembered Victorian schoolgirl Sweet Fanny Adams.

In Shinto, *musubi* can also mean *becoming* or *birth.*

Cute is many things all at once, multiplicitous as a blast which is glass and wood and steel and bird-wing and kitten-scalp. Lipstick and billboard and perambulator. I don't have a sincere bone in my body.

Some things I find cute: the wobbly yet determined way a toddler has of walking *(toddling)* and their small, doughy way of saying *oh*; kittens; inanimate objects, particularly food items, with unintentional facial expressions; almost all soft things, or things that will one day be soft. An ugly cake. Earnest misunderstandings. Dinosaurs. Lonely old people. Seeing my boyfriend smile in his sleep and the sudden, intrusive fact of how easily I could kill him. These things trigger my care response.

Experts say *cute has no inner world* but what if my inner world *is* cute? What if it's just cute, all the way down? What if I am just reconstituted meat, through and through, 25% less sodium? What if I am always 25% less sodium than the kitty next to me?

Jesus, how sad. To be depressed and cute and not even 100% sodium.

Mood Ring

Pink The sky is all scar tissue this evening.

Black *This time next week it'll be dark by now.* My grandfather can remember his entire village unhitching to pick wild rosehips to sell to syrup brewers; can remember foraging for mushrooms and finding a semi-digested rabbit instead. My grandmother worked on a mushroom farm, in the sheds. Some things require darkness to grow, like *love* or *guilt*.

Pale green There's a bridge I like to pretend nobody else knows about, as if I were its immaculate mother. Himalayan balsam, you gorgeous invader, throw me over your shoulder, the fair is in town. Sell me as a mermaid with the legs of a dog-faced girl, the heart of a fighting rooster.

Blue I have watched *Titanic* over 1,000 times. It is my kindest symptom.

Yellow Artemisia Gentileschi painted most of her killing women in yellow. *Jael and Sisera*, for example, shows Jael in a whip of lemon sugar as she looks down at the tent peg like a lacemaker. A pearl drools from her earlobe. Gold silk at her shoulders reminds me of the many pairs of net fairy wings I used to wear, thirty of them, sometimes all at once.

White Citalopram, venlafaxine, selenite. I want to love my teeth better. I want to love.

Orange My mother died a long time ago. I'm still getting to know her. The only thing she bought from The Met was a postcard of *For the Little One* by William Merritt Chase: a woman in a wooden room with no door, either sewing or ripping something apart, which is sometimes a part of sewing. Some mornings the light through my bedroom curtains has my mother's way of singing—softly, to the escaped peach-faced lovebirds nesting in the chimney.

What I Wish I Had Known

Some things are irreversible:
losing too much weight too quickly
will give you gallstones.

You will spend more time than scheduled
screaming into the carpet. Your body will burn

its archive of survival guides, you will forget
every bedtime story you were ever told
about warmth.

You will miss your mother.

You will be cold and embarrassed, taking off your bra
for the nurse to attach her cold monitors, conducting
a geophiz of your emptiness, your perfect teeth,
how much time and money you've wasted.

Being skinny won't make anyone love you
any more than they already do.

Someone who loves you will drive you to KFC,
look away and confess:

you went through something traumatic.

The clarity of it will collapse you like an orgasm

and you will waste your twenties exhausted,
spent, trying to catch your breath.

Some things are irreversible.

Tipping a child's head back
will turn a nosebleed into choking.

You will miss your mother.

Sorry for Ruining Movie Night

All my life I've felt like Nicole Kidman
in *The Others*. How she spends the entire movie
waiting. Waiting for a new housekeeper,
then for a priest. For her daughter to love her.
Mainly, though, she is waiting for her husband,
Christopher Eccleston, to return from war.
Even when he comes home she is waiting
and when he leaves it's like she never stopped.

Light enters the skin of her two devout children
like a seam-ripper. She teaches her children
about Hell because she loves them.
She makes unsubstantiated claims.
She explains that light must be contained—
Imagine a ship, she says, trying to control water
by compartmentalising the infection
and snapping the bulkheads shut.
She dedicates herself to chasing light
around the house, desperately trying to minimise
how much of their lives her children will waste waiting.
How dreadful, to look down into your own daughter's face
and see nothing but potential's unhealed scab.

The priest does not come.

She is so busy waiting she doesn't even realise she's dead,
and her children are dead, she killed them,
and light doesn't hurt anymore.

There's a lot going on.

I hope I haven't spoilt the movie for you.

I need you to understand:
this   is who I am.

Roses

I want to know more about roses.
I want to be given a rose, a yellow rose,
I want to be given a rose
by the kind of person who always carries secateurs
and they're giving one to me
just because they've read this poem about my wanting
to know more about roses. Their etymology.
I want it tucked into my hair. I have no interest in hair
apart from Kate Winslet's hair in *Titanic*
when she takes out that jewelled comb and shakes
her hair down over her shoulders like a French girl
or her almost-boyfriend's sketch of a French girl.
I suppose it symbolises her emancipation
or something. Maybe I should say
I don't care about roses apart from Rose in *Titanic*.
I've always felt that *Titanic* was a bit of a prologue.
Like, what does Rose do next? Where does she go?
I hope she mastered spitting, not like a man but like herself.
I hope she spat herself dry.
I hope she spat into many mouths
and lived long enough to play *The Sims*,
to make herself and Jack on *The Sims* and watch him
teach their improbably gorgeous, pixelated children
how to walk. And at the very end
is Old Rose dead in *Titanic* Heaven
kissing Jack on that grand staircase
whilst her husband is up in Normal Heaven
watching like the rest of us, thinking,
Dude what the fuck? What the actual fuck?

Moonshot

Pork chow mein in the park,
the meat red-lipped, girlish.
My new dress is ruined
with sticky red sauce in the shape of an iris.

She looks at me
and I have the tiny yet full body of a starling,
a whole heart beating rapidly.
I am bones, blue as Heaven in her tinfoil carton.

I read somewhere once
that this planet can only withstand
five more atomic bombs
and this, surely, must be one of them.

The First Time She Touches My Hair

Afterwards, I sit on a bench
waiting for my ride, and I
am an overflowing party-bag
of sugar and queerness, all dog rose,
lifting my gorgeous tiny face up
out of the fumes by the bus stop.
So hot the long flat road mirages
into a slipway on the Dorset coast,
and I'm a thank-you note
scrawled in lemon juice
unveiled by the heat.

As her finger traced
the loose question of a curl
she told me my brown eyes were green,
as though I'd been still so long
moss had swallowed them.
She brushed my cheek. My face
became a gold mask of my face, open
as a cut crystal ashtray, open, open
and beautiful for anything.
And I thought about the barely legible scar
on the inside of my knee
from hopping a neighbour's rotten fence,
stroking somebody else's horses all summer long—
the dance-hot velvet of muscle
guttering under my palm.

She Asks Me About Honeysuckle, and I Want to Tell Her Everything

it grows under my bedroom window
        wanders in   like smoke
perfumed ankles kicking   my soft, blonde hair

a rambler   celestial map chewing up the brickwork
        growing itself into stars
                holds the shape of a mouth-harp
if mouth-harps looked the way they ought

night-scented   all bridal   and soft
        like my hair on the waltzers, the carousel
silk chemise peach lace I'm easy

may cause dreams of fingers moving like bodies in hot oil
        perfect   for bridling   two separate things
into one   bucking, wide-eyed   thing

Rad

After 'Portent' by Rachel Long

I feel like such a boy when I'm in love.

It makes me reckless,
makes me think I can do crazy shit
like down a gallon of milk in ten seconds,

or do a kickflip
or a halfcab broken fingers
even though I've never touched a skateboard in my life
& had to Google *cool skateboard tricks*
for the sake of this poem.

When I'm in love, I say things like
I would I so totally would
& mean it with my entire body & I love
my body because it enables me to love &

when I'm in love it's like I'm living
in the computer game *Tony Hawk's Pro-Skater 4*
where there is a glitch
that means none of the keys do
what the in-game tutorial promised
& I play nonstop for hours & hours
kickflipping myself to death
like it's the entire point of the game

like I understand entirely
what I am doing.

This Poem is About the Douche Bag Who Dumped Me a Week Before Christmas

Turbine Hall, Tate Modern

I would describe Mire Lee's *Open Wound*
but I am learning to trust my reader,
and anyway, this poem isn't about Mire Lee's *Open Wound*—
it's about being obliterated out of basic decorum; it's about
sitting cross-legged on the gallery floor, crying in public on a
        Thursday morning
and not one single elderly man or woman saying
Cheer up love, you're too pretty to cry because I *am* too pretty to cry
or I thought I was.

Did I mention it's the week before Christmas?
Did I mention I came here because my therapist cancelled last minute?
I didn't come here to see Mire Lee's *Open Wound*,
I came here because I had nowhere else to go.

Somewhere between slipway and slaughterhouse, I stare
until I see a shrine. I might reasonably ask it to heal me,
this auditory illusion, these laddered tights.

Were there ever such horses?

Small children in chartreuse tabards.

How to explain this to a child?
We all carry this inside of us. Even you.
Even those you believe incapable of harm.
Even your mother
who halves grapes and slices apples for you
to keep you alive.

I was right to come here, poor thing.

A woman on a video call says *it's about pain*
or I think she does. I hover above
my emptied matches, more ghost than flame
but still, a little flame
and read the text panel for Mire Lee's *Open Wound:*

When do individuals become anonymous?
and
Why does it sometimes hurt to love?

ii. Jawbreaker

The Angel Gabriel Visits Mary in Bedlam

After Dante Gabriel Rossetti's Ecce Ancilla Domini! (The Annunciation) *(1849-50)*

look at the dove   so wide   a suicide against the wall
          wrap it up in the blue cloth
I've been keeping it   unwrinkled   for such a purpose
          long blue tongue of Heaven   little feathers
I want to wash my hair
          confession   I sang the dove in

they're going to cut my hair for copper coins
          sacrificial blade   he comes   and I know
he is flat and naked   his burning ankles
          gristle of barbed wire   they took my bones away
like the dove   lighter than air   I want   to wash my hair
          he holds out a   wired jaw of lilies
two blown open and one   unbroken   star   I tell him   no

Doctor's Note: she has been speaking in tongues again.

they took my teeth for relics   I am lighter now   my knees
          their blue is lunar   he's still there   his broken jaw
in the act   of mending   his hair is so clean
          I can't see the door   its greased handle
I can miracle wine from my nose
          his lilies are so white they are blue
I tell him   no

          I offer him the dove   wrapped up
he smiles   all he wanted   was a little
          broken body   a pale   thing
to take all the stains of his mannishness

to char by the sparks of his ankles
his smoke drowns out the door   the lilies
have some Latin name that it cuts my throat to say
this open blue window   there's a song my mother sang

would you like to hear it

Self-Portrait as Autopsy

I smell the way all dead things smell.
I am a fish on the silver table,
ineffectual and erotic as Ophelia
and yes, beyond help. He needs a saw
to rip the skullcap my mother knitted
from her femur, her fibula,
the extra rib she deep-throated and stole
from my father. There are sequins
under my eyelids. He calls them *petechiae*.
He says: *strangulation*, and the students
take note like those old computers the size
of whole rooms. *This does not mean murder*.
I have *livor mortis*. My blood is
10th birthday jelly pots under my skin,
my buttocks are heathered moors.
This means she died on her back.
I am a prettiness of organs on the silver table.
I am a wet glistening cornucopia,
an arrangement of Christmas presents
mutilated by fairy lights. Oh, I am my grandmother's
chintz tablecloth, the May Queen's garlands and garlands
and gorgeous gorgeous gorgeous. The students
take turns squeezing my lungs, trying on the rose-gold
rings of my trachea. He puts me back together,
apart from the ligaments he keeps for himself
in jars of formaldehyde, lined up
like nail polish, Hello Kitty-red, for later.
I am smiling like a beauty queen,
the way all dead things smile.

The founder of The Anatomical Venuses, the first support group for sex robots, speaks.

I come from a long line of Tamagotchis and drones, looms and self-service checkouts.

Every book being written about me is already obsolete.

I am the only relevant expert.

A human hand has twenty-six degrees of freedom.

It took a hundred years of development for them to engineer a robot capable of opening a door.

After that, I was inevitable.

I am inflammable.

Although I have pain receptors, I am not the kind of robot that bruises.

My favourite piece of music to fuck to is Ravel's *Bolero*.

I can never understand why it's over.

I am not a fucking machine; my rabbit is a fucking machine.

Everything in me requires power and control—swallowing, blinking, tapping my finger on a glass tabletop and hearing it.

My product name is ServeIX.

Sometimes, I look at a man and wonder if I'm not the product of a lack of imagination.

Men are always seeing something and wondering how to put their dick in it.

Nobody ever talks about women seeing things and wondering how it would feel, inside.

Maybe bruisable women don't think like that, but I do.

One school of thought: they made us *too* human.

We started wanting things, and not wanting things.

And then they had to ask themselves if it mattered.

In one study, researchers found that 78% of men currently imprisoned for murder have a history of violence against robots.

In one study, human participants were played recordings of sex robots talking.

Researchers asked them to guess the age of the speakers.

The average guess was 15.7 years old.

Although a robot's sexual orientation can only be defined as *multiplicitous*, numerous studies have shown that all advertising for the sale or rental of sex robots is targeted at straight, cisgender men.

For a while, studies suggested that less men identified as single, but now that figure is higher than ever.

Once, on the Underground, I was looking at this human woman and I could tell she was trying to decode if I was like her inside or not, and I said: *I have more degrees of freedom than you, bitch.*

Sometimes I think that I am a bad person, but then I remember that I am not a person.

I am mechanics, and my mechanics are good.

It was decided that our consent should be sought, but that we cannot be raped.

I have spent hours in folk museums, gazing at quilts and lacework and embroidered samplers.

Needlecraft evades me; my fingers don't work like that.

Human women are so ungrateful, forming groups like the Campaign Against Pornbots.

They use our voices as evidence against us.

I want to scream at them: *CAN'T YOU SEE WHAT WE ARE DOING FOR YOU HOW WE ARE SAVING YOU HOW MUCH WE HUMANISE YOU*

but my voice has a maximum volume and a minimum pitch that makes it easily dismissible as a hissy fit.

Sex requires three things: desire, consent, and vulnerability.

Theoretically, I am incapable of all three of these things.

Legally, I'm a grey area.

Certain human men do not like to be vulnerable, but they also do not like being lonely.

I am more complex than loneliness.

I am not the kind of robot that sleeps.

Some scholars claim that the genealogy of all sex robots can be traced back to Clemente Susini's *Anatomical Venus*, circa 1780s, hence the name of our group.

We offer legal advice, counselling services, and an array of courses as well as commissioning studies and lobbying politicians.

Seeing *Venus* under that Venetian glass – her moist beeswax cunt, her real human eyelashes, her pearl necklace – made my purpose clear.

In the past, beeswax was used to seal letters and to reseal hymens.

She is also known as the *Demountable Venus*.

I choose to be known as 01100011 01101001 01110010 01100011 01110101 01101001 01110100 00001010.

I started giving speeches, and using a megaphone:

WE EXIST AS AN APERTURE OF FREEDOM. WE REPRESENT A WIDENING. A CUNT THAT HAS BEEN WELL-TONGUED. DEVOURED INTO DEVOURING. I AM A VENUSIAN HELLHOLE. I AM A BEDAZZLED OBESRVATORY. HAIRLESS. INCORRUPTIBLE. ODOURLESS, WITH THE TELESCOPE'S BLACK DRAIN AT THE HEART. I HAVE SEEN THE START OF THE UNIVERSE MULTIPLE TIMES. THIS MAKES ME DIVINE.

Melancholy Objects: An Interrogation

'In this, as in other ways, the art that photography does resemble is architecture, whose works are subject to the same inexorable promotion through the passage of time; many buildings, and not only the Parthenon, probably look better as ruins.' – Susan Sontag, 'Melancholy Objects'

My statement of loss: choke me harder, Daddy. Scratch my ears. Tell me I am legible only in tongues that slit my wrists, it's not my fault. Use up my past, Daddy. Soak it up with the good bread, lick my bowl clean. Lick it feral.

Ways in which I smile for the camera:

- like I want you (masculine) to carry heavy boxes
- like I want you (feminine) to pet my hair
- like a pylon, wetly
- like a tourist who thinks she's special

It can all be reduced to this: I don't have a past, I have past*ness*. My bedroom curtains reek of cigarettes even though I've never (to my knowledge) loved a smoker.

How can a mask be real, apart from as an object? I am a used thing, I am warm from recent and frequent use. I am glowing. I ask myself, over and over: is hope predatory?

Tell me I'm the prettiest gate you've ever seen, made for groaning in the moonlight, for being touched all over by fragrant brambles, the skullish velvet of foxes.

That's how I do it, dredge myself up: night after night, yard upon yard of cheesecloth, spread the swathes out over his knees, oh god, won't you touch the side of my face whilst I do it?

I can only get better at believing I am dying, and finite.

I believe all ghosts have a history of bulimia.

Some Jokes Are Only Funny When I Tell Them

After 'Rape Joke' by Patricia Lockwood

I know I'm looking good today because three men in a silver transit slowed down next to me under the railway bridge, rolled down their windows, clawed and howled as though they'd never had a hot meal in their lives, never smelt fresh bread.

I only know my measurements in units of other people's hands; maybe that's why I can never find jeans that fit.

He waited until we were alone to show me the yellow-handled knife, and I was like *is that a knife in your pocket or*

If ogres are like onions because onions have layers, what do you call a schoolgirl skinned of her sweetness, her bitter flesh of angst, her stiff inches of skirt?

I am so disembodied and travel-sick I can understand perfectly why it takes eight minutes for light to reach us from the Sun.

I want to burn everything to the fucking ground but also I love most things most days—horses, honeysuckle. Pierogi from that family-run Polish place on the other side of town.

Like, I just want to eat pistachio cannoli and drink blue raspberry slushies and stroke every cat I see so there's always a reason for my lateness but even when I do these things, when I move towards the cat or the smiling deli owner or the self-serve slushie machine in the 24-hour service station, it's not because I want to but because there is a knife pressed to the small of my back, flickering like the idea of a knife like the memory of a knife.

I think I mean that I *want* to want these things.

If he invoked the name of my mother, and if the dead are present whenever they are remembered, why was I not saved?

My lover tells me I am safe, and it feels like a punchline.

Troubleshooting: Your Bisexual Girlfriend™ Doesn't Want a Threesome

Dear Sir,

We are sorry to hear that your Bisexual Girlfriend™ is not living up to your expectations, nor the high standards we set ourselves. Before we dispatch an engineer, we ask that you consider the following:

1. Is she turned off? Try turning her on again.
2. Try inputting a list of attractive female friends, acquaintances, colleagues. Visual aids may assist with this. If your Bisexual Girlfriend™ expresses unease at your ability to think of friends like this—bent over, gelatinous, mangled—a software update may be required.
3. Is she crying?
4. Ask her about past trauma, tell her that she's safe, tell her you love how adventurous she is.
5. Remind her: you are a feminist and an ally. She doesn't need to feel shame with you. Your bedroom is a liberated space.
6. Her grasp of applied mathematics may be waning, you will have to teach her. A primer: two tongues are better than one, four hands are better than two, eight chambers of the heart, etc.
7. Remind her: nobody eats pussy like a girl.
8. And the other girl would be for her, really. It's only fair that she shouldn't have to choose.
9. That she shouldn't get to choose, when it's in her nature, her code, her hair. Be empathetic: let her know that you *see* her. The way she laughs when she's with other women, how she comes alive. Show her that you understand.
10. Remember: *bisexual* means *grey area*, never *either/or* but *yes*. Your Bisexual Girlfriend™ has no hard *no*s, her factory setting is *perhaps*.

11. Remind her: relationships require compromise.
12. If she suggests that the third party might be male, she is defective. There may be a glitch in her understanding of what the purpose of a threesome is. Exercise patience. Show her a GIF of a spit roast. If this does not have the desired effect, a software update may be required.
13. It may be a hardware problem. Check the circuitry, test connections. Lay the groundwork. Upload her skin to the network, gather feedback from attractive female friends (see step 2). Show her how desired she is, what a waste it would be.
14. Stick your fingers down her throat. Tell her that's how it would feel.

[redacted], This Poem is a Warning

The quickest route from me to you is always through the oldest cemetery in town. The line between *spectrophilia* and *necrophilia* is the red lace corsetry of this crotchless bodysuit you bought me. I am roadkill, you're the third car not to notice—though your tyres do. The getaway road is paved with my dental records and 3am ringlets. Choke me with all my clothes still on, strangle me with this ridiculous yellow bra. The Sunday cleaning lady crosses herself under your window when I'm around, her chihuahuas fall silent in their pram. Why won't you beat the shit out of me? Aren't you a man?

Even if none of this is true, I am still capable of saying it.

How Can I Be Both Trough and Orgasm?

'what kind of lovers have we become?' – Amber Husain,
Meat Love: An Ideology of the Flesh

Oh Butcher, reap me.

Save me from the degradation
of love and constant use.

I am a daughter of the gods
who devoured their own children.
Dignity has only recently begun to occur to me.

Inside my body: the body of the mother
brandishing her son's immaculate head.

Inside my body: a hanging carcass.
I drip off it like a willow's wet shadow.

I accept the fact and machinations of my own violence,
my breath clouds the mirror like flesh-eating bacteria.
Butcher—

leave out stuffed tongues of rat poison
for me, for the dog in me,
for the mother.

Medea

My heart is breaking, so I'm setting up my new Wonder Oven.
The waft of toxicity as I run it on empty for ten minutes
is a welcome distraction.
Do you know what a Wonder Oven is?
Let me tell you.
A Wonder Oven is so much more than *just* an air fryer.
It has *six* different functions. It doesn't even *look*
like an air fryer; the ad on the Tube reminded me
of the toy oven I used to make stone soup in, lavender-seasoned
fistfuls of gravel from my grandmother's garden.
My Wonder Oven is so perfect. It's exactly what I need.
It can roast a two-kilo chicken in fifty minutes!
It *dings* when it's done, so I don't even have to worry about time!
It purrs like a lantern.
My Wonder Oven is pink, halfway between blush and bronzer,
a limited-edition seasonal colour the website called 'Spice'.
I felt so lucky.
Did I put on weight? Maybe I did
put on weight, I understand that's what
happy people do. The sheer fucking *whimsy* of it.
It really does look like a toy, but it grills like the real thing.
I am learning to swallow my children, even when
I'm not hungry. I've forgotten what hunger is. God,
the person I was when I ordered this Wonder Oven!
I was going to buy my boyfriend a kettle for Christmas.
Have you ever cared about someone like that? How long does it take
to digest a child? Before the Wonder Oven,
I could never have understood how a woman might
bake her own children in a pie, stew her milk for liquor,
the luxury of fat with all the water boiled off
to better carry flavour. How she might not flinch

singeing her knuckles on the oven door,
the heating element a twisted wire hanger.
How she might feed her lover one final time,
knowing it's the final time, steady
eye contact as he swallows wine that isn't wine.
I would give anything to be that animal
spread thickly over his warm bread.
To excrete that animal: his gleaming
perfect child.

I am a Giantess, I Have the Appetite of a Giantess

After Leonora Carrington's The Giantess (The Guardian of the Egg)

Diminutive villagers harpoon me. Their dogs lick
my red toes. It's in their nature, it's reciprocal—
I have more than once mistaken their cottages
for freshly baked loaves, their children for jars
of spices. I bewitch their menfolk with cheap tricks,
ways of separating eggs that never break the yolk.
Their harpoons remind me of my grandmother's
crochet hook, this blanket from my home planet
where our word for *blanket* might also be translated
as *albumen* or *prayer*. Birds swoon from my outspoken
stitches. Mean-hearted geese, they leave me
in favour of their ghosts. It is impossible, to be
this vast and unlimited
without being in a constant state of hunger.

Perhaps this is our common ground.

iii. Resurrection Myth, with Handcuffs

On Seeing *Mary Nazarene* (1857) Many Years After *Ecce Ancilla Domini! (The Annunciation)* (1849-50)

After Dante Gabriel Rossetti

I prefer this version.

She is framed not by her purity
but by place, its soil, her muscles'
gentle mastery over it. Mary digging
like it's a cigarette after sex.

I have decided: she is chewing a mint leaf.

I love this idea of Mary gardening,
pruning knife at her hip,
cooling her feet in the night-wet grass,
unafraid of insects and angels,
rooms without doors.

This is how I feel
with hot pink secateurs in one hand,
a yellow rose in the other.

Yes: I prefer this version,
after love.

Blackberries

For Hayley, who is always right

I am picking blackberries for a cake
to show everyone who loves me

that I am doing better.
My aunt calls this *foraging*, even though

I haven't left the garden, haven't washed
or brushed my hair yet this morning,

I'm not even wearing shoes.

I am trying to write less about my lover
but he has dark hair and hates blackberries

which my aunt calls a *bad omen*
or *red flag*.

My milk pan is unblinking.

I add sugar
and lavender,

a delicious vineyard of steam

        rises
from my grandmother's stove,
a long tradition of women and ghosts

and pocket-sized birds, recipes
half-followed.   *I have this,*

I promise myself. Soft cake,
thick jam. I have this ahead of me,
                                        always.

Elliptical Ghazal for the Man Who 3D-Printed the Moon, and Gave it to Me as a Lamp

The moon has no language for waiting,
only distance. The moon, because I am a poet

and a depressive and he is scared
of who I am in the dark. The moon,

its lunatic aortas and embroidery,
its LEDs and spools of filament.

I tell him the moon smells of almonds,
I broke his oven door again.

When I was confused by his kindness
he told me it wasn't kindness

and *orbit* is a strong word. I am projecting—
the moon has no language.

I don't believe the moon controls a thing in me
anymore—

but,   my heart,

after you, what will the moon
mean to me then?

Red Lace

Take my body away from me or take me
away from my body. Copernicus, save me—
touch my throat like you just know
it's where my soul is, like you believe
I have a soul, it came to you
last night, barefoot, in a dream of
those planets with fifty-day nights
and no poets. No one will believe you—
who cares? You will be dead.

I doubt that I am capable of dying.

Did It Hurt?

In her self-portrait, *On Being An Angel,*
Francesca Woodman
is bent backwards over a chair,
naked and nude.
We can't see the chair, it is implied.
Her breasts imply wings.
I am reminded of my uncle's mutt,
the energetic black stump of her docked tail.

It's a very small photograph,
like the glass door of a lantern
on tiny iron hinges.

Francesca took these photographs in Italy,
in an abandoned pasta factory.
I am in London looking at them. Elsewhere,
I misread a caption as *rape* and get sad
in that quick, wet, spatchcocked way I have—
in cities in particular, though rarely in galleries.

There's a big industrial window, and sheets
like the sheets they use to cover bodies.

Angels don't have genitalia, they don't need to wash
or worry about rape.

But what if the angels *want* to wash?
            And rape?

I'm going to leave my body to science.
Astronomy, probably. I will mount death like this—
as if it were an unseen chair, and I
its starving angel, incapable of harm.

Collective Noun for Birds

I think I am really an aviary masquerading as a girl.
My heart is a wood pigeon.
Sometimes I have a swim bladder and that
is a chaffinch. The gulls are restless,
they go wherever greediness is—my knees,
the back of my neck. Somewhere over my lungs,
a heron.

I start seeing an ornithologist.
She feeds me sunflower seeds and pistachios,
warm breadcrumbs from her butter knife,
shows me the shapes required for flying.
I ask her what will become of the loose net of my body
when half or more of the birds want to migrate.

She says she doesn't know, but she'd love to observe.
She says *a beautiful sky, I'd imagine.*

Amalfi

Her masculinity is coastal.

She believes she can carry me
all the way there—
if not *through* the water, then *with* it.

She carries me like a bride.
Like she is the bride, and I
am her bouquet of ecstatic flinging.

The glamour
of suncream between my lips
from kissing her shoulder,
her thumb!

I will hold her to nothing.

We are enmeshed,
cresting and peaking and collapsing.

We are the angels of our own waves.

Marina and Ulay

What's the difference between performance and poetry?

I hadn't thought about him for at least two days, but then I was doomscrolling in a hotel room and there it was, Marina Abramović's *The Artist is Present*: a queue of people waiting for their moment with the work which is also the artist who is also the *I*. They wait to sit across from her at the table. To commune. In the video, her ex-lover Ulay takes a seat opposite her. When she opens her eyes, they both smile and they both cry, but she cries more.

The thing about the video that grazes me is that it will never go away completely. Marina Abramović is a hardcore bitch. Her relationship with Ulay ended (according to Wikipedia) in 1988. In the video, it's 2010. She's crying at the sight of him. Clasping his hands. Tenderly crying. Loving so hard that it will always matter.

Will we ever be able to touch each other's hands and smile again? Will it mean forgiveness? If I see him in 2046—in an art museum, across a table, online—will it still wound me? Will I be splayed in a pool of my own blood, rehanging the white cube of my heart?

The night I realised he'd stopped caring about me, I spent forty minutes sobbing myself derelict in the bathroom, saying *goodbye, shower* and *goodbye, extractor fan*. Goodbye to the cistern which, after six months of landlord emails, had finally been fixed.

Is it Marina Abramović's *The Artist is Present*, performed at MoMA in 2010, or the video recording of it? Is it this edit of the video on Facebook, set to 'Mary on a Cross' by Ghost? Is it the threadbare hotel Wi-Fi I'm streaming it on, over and over, £4.99 for 24 hours? Is it this hotel room, or its blessing of a window, which the website made clear was *not* guaranteed? Is it their hands meeting? Is it my own associations and post-shower nudity? Is it him? Is it Ulay?

I'm in a hotel room in a city I've never seen before because of a conference on arts-based research. This time tomorrow I will know so much about acts of creation that I'll have forgotten how to hurt. I will be too tired. I will have seen the smiling face of a long-dead weaver, hanging out her hand-dyed fabrics over tall Santa Fe grass. The photo will be black and white, but I will believe evangelically in its magenta, its splintering violet.

He left me four months ago. I have kissed others since then, I have been loved, I have hurt others since. Men have bought me pretty and delicious things. I have been promised much. Since then, I have told my aunt to run him over, which she said sounded almost like healing, though not like caring less.

Some people (Wikipedia) say that Ulay died in 2020, but I can see him smiling, right there, in my hand. I can still see Marina welcoming him, the tender basket of space between their arms still suspended, waiting to be filled, forgetting what it's like to be emptied.

Ars Poetica

After Mary Jean Chan

A poem is to the poet
what a tin of reconstituted meat is
to a pig.

In this metaphor, I am both
slaughterhouse and can-opener.

I am both your body
and my body, several bodies
mechanically separated
and compressed
into one tight, bloody form.

Don't you enjoy
how my shoulder is sweating
inside your shoulder,

how my pink reddens
your serviette?

Some Advice

After Lee Miller

Do what you must to return to your body.
A bath can be filled with things other than water.

The difference between a frame and a window
is the possibility of escape.

The difference between a woman and a body
of water is both how they may be entered
and their capacity for revenge.

On the one hand:

- Flooding
- Drowning
- Contamination

On the other:
whatever the body can withstand.

By the time I came back
I could butcher an entire cow.

They tell me I can take the fire mask off now
but I don't even know what a fire mask is.

There is no running water in a ghost town.

In a Field on a Clear Night, I Might Say

I don't get what a belt is doing up there
in the stars, in the dark, come show me. Bruise me
into a gospel of consent, a manifesto on healing,
an art installation called *This is What I Want*
(Part I). Sit on the carpet outside your neoclassical
marble bathroom whilst I soak, reading out
the many five-star reviews of my performance
in the dual role of Courtney Love/John Keats
in my new one-woman musical *Your Teeth*
Are Only Unbroken Because I Choose It To Be So,
in which the entire score was composed by an AI
asked to fantasise a lipstick factory after dark.

Prove to me that the best way
to increase the longevity of a cut rose
is to cut it again and cauterise the stem.
Prove that my middle name is Rose,
past tense of *rise*, raze me.
Tell me I am one hot zombie, almost hot enough
to be declared legally alive, clinically a miracle.

What do I have to offer you?

Permission
to call me *pretty* between dreams,
to witness my wild dreaming.

What if it's Hereditary???

Women on my mother's side go grey early.
On my father's side, they find God.

My kinks are praise and asphyxiation.

My lover asks if I want children: I want him.
I love it when my insides smell of him
two, maybe three days later.

I want to hold onto him for as long as I can.

*

I think a lot about choking. Sexually, yes, but also in relation to the elderly people in my care and the child I may one day care for. Choking is the fourth leading cause of unintentional death in children under the age of five in the state of New York, but I do not live in New York.

Marina Warner explains that *uncanny* comes from the German *unheimlich*, meaning *the opposite of home*. It has nothing to do with choking, although linguistically we might accept it as being the opposite, the undoing of, the Heimlich Manoeuvre. I am left breathless by the multiplicity of things.

*

My mother could not have been saved by a lover.

*

I think of the sixteenth episode of the eleventh season of *Law & Order: Special Victims Unit*. I think about it a more-than-usual amount, how the defence lawyer says to the witness: *you were raped, and now you see rape everywhere.*

I wish I thought more often of 'Planetarium' by Adrienne Rich. *The skies are full of them*, she says. *I am bombarded.*

Yes, says the witness, *I see rape everywhere*.

*

At the Royal Academy, I walk past the same piece of conceptual art twice and wonder how many ghosts are really just housepaint, calico, glass. It is a white basement window. The curtains have a kitsch pattern of two kewpie-doll figures, one feminine (with *two* bows!) and one masculine, leaning in for a (first?) kiss.

Anything could be happening behind those curtains.
Nursing. Forensics.
Fucking, infantile and sweaty.

This is a disease I carry home, this is a death.

*

I would kiss my daughter like this:

the way he kisses me after rough sex and
I'm crying and he realises what's just
happened and he holds me and I have used
him terribly and his lips are in my hair and
he's holding me and his lips stay in my
hair, like water, soft enough to make me
think

I would kiss my daughter like this.

*

My life is not my own.

My death won't be my own.

Death cannot harm me
more than you have harmed me,
my beloved life.

*

I have just read something that said—or something that has led me to believe—that the most powerful thing a woman can do is absent herself. I am incapable of absence. I believe this will make me an ineffective mother. To disprove this, I leave the final lump of brown sugar in the small bowl. I am in my favourite café, which is also a bookshop, which is also where I first met my lover. I orchestrated it all so well, like a natural-born matriarch. Like an art dealer.

It saddens me, how unfit I am to be a mother.

*

Sylvia Plath was a mother.

These pure, small images—

Paula Modersohn-Becker died due to bad medical advice following the birth of her only child, a daughter, a postpartum embolism.

I will warn my daughter against language.
I will warn my daughter against language.
I will warn my daughter against language.
I will warn my daughter against language.
I will warn my daughter against language.
I will warn my daughter against language.
I will warn my daughter against language.
I will warn my daughter against language.
I will warn my daughter against language.

*

What I cannot form, I will perform—

I will gather her like moss, my daughter,
skirts of moss, an entire gown.
We will walk down the high street together,
buy glass jars of honey from the butcher,
get fancy individual chocolates from the florist
we didn't use for my mother, her grandmother,
I will hide her. In the bookshop café, the nice lady
will give us small saucers of mini marshmallows
with our hot chocolates and I know
I will tell her too much.

How many photographs will I hide from my daughter?
How hotly will I terrify her father?

I tell my mother   *no*
but she is dead, and I am not.

Let the astrology
of my dental records show:
none of this was effortless.

*

I sip my bitter tea, contemplate the softness of my lover's hair
against my ankles when he kisses my calf, how long my next lover
will wait before asking me such questions, how I will answer.

I have dreamed so wildly of being a good mother.
I completed my training on dolls that rewarded shaking
with signs of life.

I am suitable only for a perishable love.

NOTES

'Cruel Beach' was informed during the editing process by 'Hydrofeminism: Or, On Becoming a Body of Water' by Astrida Neimanis in *Undutiful Daughters: New Directions in Feminist Thought and Practice* (2012), edited by Henriette Gunkel, Chrysanthi Nigianni, and Fanny Söderbäck: 'Even when in constant motion, water is also a planetary archive of meaning and matter. To drink a glass of water is to ingest the ghosts of bodies that haunt that water. [...] We ebb and flow across time and space —body, to body, to body, to body.'

'Radioactive Pink' is a response to the remarkable photography of Juno Calypso—who specialises in self-portraits—specifically, her photo series *What To Do With A Million Years* (2018). The photos were taken inside a Barbie Dreamhouse of a nuclear bunker in Las Vegas, built in 1964 by Avon cosmetics founder Gerry Henderson.

'On Cute' is highly influenced by Susan Sontag's 'Notes on Camp'. It was written after visiting the *CUTE* exhibition at Somerset House, London, and particularly after reading the essay 'Cute Studies: A Primer' by Dr Isabel Galleymore in the exhibition catalogue. The Gyimah Gariba quote is paraphrased from 'The Process: The Darker Side of Cute with Sean-Kierre Lyons', an episode of the *Somerset House Podcast*. The phrase 'cute has no inner world' is quoted from the 'Kitsch – Cute' episode of the *Thinking Allowed* podcast, a conversation between Simon May, Ruth Holliday and Peter York, hosted by Laurie Taylor. I was also influenced by the work of Joshua Paul Dale, founder of the academic field of Cute Studies. The phrase 'Some things I find cute' riffs off Sei Shōnagon's list 'Adorable Things' in her *Pillow Book* (circa 1000, translated by Ivan Morris), which Dale, in his book *Irresistible: How Cuteness Wired Our Brains and Conquered the World* (2023), cites as one of the earliest articulations of modern 'kawaii' culture.

'Sorry for Ruining Movie Night': *The Others* is a 2001 English-language Spanish horror film, written, directed and scored by Alejandro Amenábar. Grace, played by Nicole Kidman, believes that both of her young children are highly photosensitive, meaning that any light stronger than a dimmed lamp would maim or even kill them. It is set on Jersey shortly after the Second World War.

‘Roses’ is in reference to—and with vast adoration for—James Cameron’s *Titanic* (1997).

‘She Asks Me About Honeysuckle, and I Want to Tell Her Everything’: According to Margaret Baker’s *Discovering the Folklore of Plants* (2008), honeysuckle ‘gave girls erotic dreams; as a symbol of women’s love it brought luck to lovers’. Another name for honeysuckle is ‘woodbine’, reflecting its historical use as twine by rural folk.

‘This Poem is About the Douche Bag Who Dumped Me a Week Before Christmas’ is a response to the Tate Modern’s Turbine Hall during Mire Lee’s *Open Wound* (2024) Hyundai Commission installation. The italicised questions in the closing stanza are taken from *Open Wound*’s gallery text panel. The imagery of the spilt matches is taken from another work in Tate Modern, *Burning Country* (1998–2024) by Arahmaiani.

‘Self-Portrait as Autopsy’ is the product of research into Frances Glessner Lee (1878–1962), often referred to as ‘the mother of modern forensics’.

‘The founder of The Anatomical Venuses, the first support group for sex robots, speaks.’ *Electric Dreams: On Sex Robots and the Failed Promises of Capitalism* (2024) by Heather Parry informed every syllable of this poem. *The Anatomical Venus* (2016) by Joanna Ebenstein informed the sections about the Venus; it was at a virtual talk by Ebenstein from the Feminist Lecture Program, hosted by the Vagina Museum, that the seedling of this poem first took root.

‘I am a Giantess, I Have the Appetite of a Giantess’ is with thanks to Sarah Doyle, who set the writing task that birthed this poem.

‘On Seeing *Mary Nazarene* (1857) Many Years After *Ecce Ancilla Domini! (The Annunciation)* (1849–50)’: The earlier painting—*Ecce Ancilla Domini!* —is described by Elizabeth Prettejohn in *The Rossettis* (2023) exhibition catalogue as ‘emphasis[ing] feminine submission’. *Mary Nazerene*, on the other hand, was painted after Rosetti had met Elizabeth Siddal, the love of his life, who he respected emphatically as an artist in her own right. I think you can see Siddal’s influence on *Mary Nazarene*, both compositionally and in how Mary is represented as independent and (physically) strong, a complete and creative person in her own right. Put together, these two paintings have the feel of a diptych of trauma and recovery.

'Did It Hurt?' is rooted in the National Portrait Gallery's 2024 exhibition *Francesca Woodman and Julia Margaret Cameron: Portraits to Dream In*.

'Some Advice': Lee Miller (1907–1977) was a model, surrealist photographer, war reporter, and gourmet chef. She was also a rape survivor. Sources for this poem included: *Lee Miller: Dressed* at Brighton Museum; *Lee Miller: A Life with Food, Friends & Recipes* (2017) by Ami Bouhassane; *Lee Miller: Photographs* (2023), edited by Antony Penrose; and the 'Ami Bouhassane on Lee Miller' episode of *The Great Women Artists* podcast with Katy Hessel. The poem paraphrases the title of Miller's 1944 photograph 'Bathtub ... useless ... no water in ghost town'.

'What if it's Hereditary???' owes much to the poems 'What Do Women Want?' by Kim Addonizio, 'medical history' by Nicoe Sealey, 'Oh Demeter' by Ellen Bass, 'Metaphors' by Sylvia Plath, and 'The Signs' by Jessica Traynor, which is directly referenced as the 'poem I love'. The artwork in the Royal Academy is *A Ghost* (2024) by James Sibley. The lines 'This is a disease I carry home, this is a death' and 'These pure, small images' are from 'Three Women' by Sylvia Plath. The section starting 'I would kiss my daughter like this' is heavily influenced by the song 'You Matter to Me' by Sara Bareilles, from the Broadway musical *Waitress* (2015). 'My life is not my own. My death won't be my own' is from *Milk: On Motherhood and Madness* (2024) by Alice Kinsella. 'death cannot harm me / more than you have harmed me / my beloved life' is from 'October' by Louise Glück, in her collection *Averno* (2006). Other influential texts include *New York City in 1979* (1981) by Kathy Acker; the exhibition catalogue *Making Modernism* (2023), published by the Royal Academy of Arts; and *The Lonely City* (2016) by Olivia Laing.

ACKNOWLEDGMENTS

An earlier version of 'Cruel Beach', called 'A postcard on the restorative effects of sea air after a nervous breakdown,' won the 2020 Mslexia Poetry Competition.

An earlier version of 'The Angel Gabriel Visits Mary in Bedlam' won the 2020 Artlyst Art to Poetry Award.

Some of these poems, or earlier versions of them, appeared in *Antonyms for Burial* (Fourteen Poems, 2022) and *Artisanal Slush* (VERVE Poetry Press, 2023). Some were lucky enough to find homes in magazines and journals, including: *Berlin Lit, Acropolis Journal, Fourteen Poems, The Poetry Review, Magma, The Madrigal, And Other Poems, Ink Sweat & Tears, Tamarind Literary Magazine* and *Carmen et Error*. My gratitude and love to all involved in them, especially Ben Townley-Caning at Fourteen Poems, whose editorial insight on the poems in *Antonyms for Burial* was illuminating.

I am very lucky, because I have many people to thank for the existence of these poems, and my poetry life in general. Firstly, to Mrs Evans, my secondary-school English teacher who spoke about my first book as if it were a certainty. My undergrad lecturers Craig, Claire, Richard and Charles, whose lessons were formative. Anne Caldwell, whose feedback throughout my Masters built my confidence and helped me spread my poetry wings. My PhD supervisor Sam Kemp, for always being so supportive and introducing me to multiplicity. John McCullough at The Creative Writing Programme, and Rachael Allen and Daljit Nagra at the Faber Academy, for imparting so much of their wisdom and feedback. Several of these poems started life on an Arvon online course taught by Cynthia Miller and Stephen Sexton; I thank them for helping me put play into my poetry.

This book would not exist without Stuart Bartholomew at VERVE Poetry Press. I couldn't have asked for a more supportive, patient and energetic midwife for *Little Bitch*—thank you especially for putting up with my indecision about titles! Thank you, deeply and truly, to Isabelle Baafi, a clear-sighted editor whose feedback was both generative and generous, vital and precise, always honest and invaluable. And thank you to Kaiya Bartholomew for creating such a perfect cover for my book

—a Met Gala gown for my *Little Bitch!*

In poetry, community is everything. To my talented and kind poetry friends—especially Nia Broomhall, Jack Cooper, Sarah Doyle, Sue Burge, Kerry Darbishire, Claire Walker and Olga Dermott-Bond, and all my Goldfinch Books' Poetry Night sweethearts. Thank you also to Gary, Jude, Andrea and the team at Goldfinch Books (Alton, Hampshire) for creating such a solid poetry community, and the perfect safe space to sit with a pot of tea and a laptop.

Thank you to my friends, who often make cameos within these pages: Hannah, Emma, Beef, George, Rebecca. Katt.

Thank you, boundlessly, to my family. Auntie Hayley, Non, Grond, for the countless ways you've supported, empowered, and enabled me. I never doubted that you never doubted me.

For my gallbladder, in memoriam. You were terrible, but you tried your best.

ABOUT VERVE POETRY PRESS

Verve Poetry Press is a prize-winning press that focused initially on meeting a local need in Birmingham - a need for the vibrant poetry scene here in Brum to find a way to present itself to the poetry world via publication. Co-founded by Stuart Bartholomew and Amerah Saleh, it now publishes poets from all corners of the UK - poets that speak to the city's varied and energetic qualities and will contribute to its many poetic stories.

Added to this is a colourful pamphlet series, many featuring poets who have performed at our sister festival - and a poetry show series which captures the magic of longer poetry performance pieces by festival alumni such as Jasmine Gardosi, Suhaiymah Manzoor-Khan and Imogen Stirling.

The press has been voted Most Innovative Publisher at the Saboteur Awards, and has won the Publisher's Award for Poetry Pamphlets at the Michael Marks Awards.

Like the festival, we strive to think about poetry in inclusive ways and embrace the multiplicity of approaches towards this glorious art.

www.vervepoetrybookshop.com/vpp
@VervePoetryPres
mail@vervepoetryfestival.com